F-111
AARDVARK
Anthony M. Thornborough

Front cover illustration: An RDT&E F-111A salvoes two dozen Mk 82 'slicks'. Note the multiple ejection bomb-racks, later replaced by more streamlined bomb-release units. (General Dynamics)

Back cover illustrations.
Top: Plattsburgh's thirty-six FB-111As wear artwork on the fuselage sides, considered by many ground crews to be the finest examples in the USAF today, applied in miniature by airbrush. 68-0289 is nicknamed 'Queen Hi' and 68-0251 is christened 'Shy-Chi Baby'. (USAF)

Below: A 20th TFW F-111E displays its upper camouflage pattern while at its optimum cruise height of about 22,000ft. The USAF is presently experimenting with a new series of decors for the One-Elevens, and major changes to the Vietnam night scheme, now used for some twenty years, are afoot. (USAF)

1. The variant that made it to the prototype stage but which was subsequently cancelled by Prime Minister Wilson and never flew in RAF markings: the F-111K. This General Dynamics artist's rendition depicts two F-111Ks in loose formation equipped with 600USgal wing tanks and 1,000lb bombs. The F-111K most closely resembled the RAAF F-111C structurally, but was to be equipped with the advanced, solid-state MkII avionics used in the USAF F-111D. (General Dynamics)

F-111
AARDVARK

Anthony M. Thornborough

ARMS AND
ARMOUR

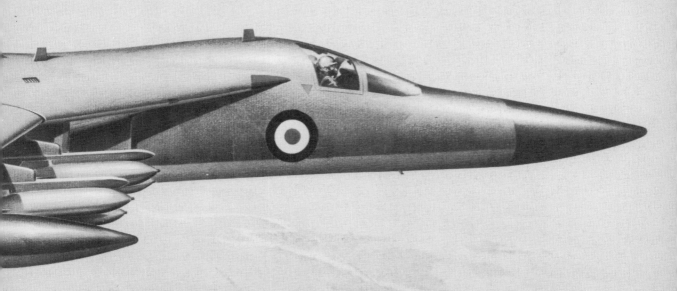

INTRODUCTION

First published in Great Britain in 1989 by Arms and Armour Press, Artillery House, Artillery Row, London SW1P 1RT.

Distributed in the USA by Sterling Publishing Co. Inc., 2 Park Avenue, New York, NY 10016.

Distributed in Australia by Capricorn Link (Australia) Pty. Ltd., P.O. Box 665, Lane Cove, New South Wales 2066, Australia.

British Library Cataloguing in Publication Data:
Thornborough, Anthony M.
F-111 Aardvark
1. General Dynamics F-111 aeroplanes
I. Title II. Series
623.74'64
ISBN 0-85368-935-0

Line illustrations by the author.

Designed and edited by DAG Publications Ltd.
Designed by David Gibbons; layout by Cilla Eurich; typeset by Ronset Typesetters Ltd, Darwen, Lancashire, and Typesetters (Birmingham) Ltd, Warley, West Midlands; camerawork by M&E Reproductions, North Fambridge, Essex; printed and bound in Great Britain by The Alden Press, Oxford.

2. 380th BW FB-111A on the hardstand at Plattsburgh AFB, prior to launch. One-Eleven radomes are distinctly glossy. (USAF)

Not a fighter, and not a fully-fledged heavy bomber either, the General Dynamics F-111 falls into the unique category of dedicated interdictor. Capable of flying nap-of-the-earth in all weathers at transonic speeds with a warload unsurpassed by all but the 'heavies', the One-Eleven – popularly known as the 'Aardvark' but more commonly referred to in USAF circles as 'The Cadillac of the Air Force' – is something very special. True, its air-to-air capabilities are limited to a 20mm 'gat' and short-range all-aspect AIM-9 missiles, and its primary role is that of 'hauling iron' – bombing. But potential enemies have more than a passing respect for that MiG-killing weaponry and anyone who has watched One-Elevens 'shoot patterns', performing hard wing-overs around the swing-wingers' home-'dromes, would be hard pressed to think of it as anything other than an attack machine with a considerable sting.

Excluding the short-lived Navy variant, from its inception during the Tactical Fighter Experimental (TFX) programme of the early 1960s through to very recent times the One-Eleven has stuck to one major role: attack behind the Forward Edge of the Battle Area. Progressive upgrades to avionics and weapons kits have since enabled the family to branch out and take on such new assignments as strategic missile launcher, selective and barrage radar-jamming in support of airborne 'friendlies', armed recce, anti-shipping missileer, *standoff* 'smart' bombing, and even Battlefield Area Interdiction and Close Air Support in league with Special Forces; and doing those jobs using a whole range of more dynamic flying modes.

In many respects, the true potential of the Aardvark has not yet been fully explored. The pioneering technology General Dynamics introduced so courageously – variable geometry wings, afterburning turbofans, a crew escape module, tactical 'blind' bombing avionics offering 'uncanned' attack profiles, and automatic terrain following flight systems – were subject to some minor teething problems blown out of all proportion by the popular media. Added to this were a spate of crashes in 1968–9 related to design or quality control problems, resulting in a prolonged grounding order which delayed entry of the F-111C into RAAF service, the sole export customer, by five years. However, General Dynamics had the problems well in hand and proved it by demonstrating the Aardvark's ability to remain structurally sound for a *hundred years'* worth of operational flying!; the hiccups were cured very early in life and the type has since gone on to accrue a truly remarkable combat record over South East Asia and Libya; it has also formed one of the strongest links in America's nuclear deterrence both from home and at forward bases in Europe. Moreover, at the time of writing, the type had flown well over one million flying hours, and enjoys a super safety record. But for unknown reasons the early TFX stigma was hard to shake off, and, only now, as ex-swing-wing crews rise to the higher echelons of the user air forces, the USAF and RAAF, are the F-111s being deployed to maximum effect. Destined to serve well into the 1990s, the Aardvark will doubtless continue in its present roles and take on many others, as more and more One-Eleven crews get to call the shots; and so valuable have the aircraft become that General Dynamics is presently engaged in restoring several previously written-off 'basket cases' (damaged aircraft) back to full operational capability.

Comparisons with the much newer and comparatively petite Anglo-German-Italian Tornado interdictor are inevitable. RAF Tornado crews, who have demonstrated remarkable prowess by beating some of America's best bomber crews at competition level, tend to forget that the 'Earth Pig' (the F-111's less flattering nickname) was bulling its way through valleys peppered with AAA and dropping ordnance smack on target 'in the weather' when Tornado had barely attained drawing-board status. And today, twenty years later, the large rugged airframe of the F-111 is hard to beat when it comes to range, payload, and internal, low-drag countermeasures systems. Furthermore, a massive avionics upgrade is quietly taking place, converting the vintage F-111A/E models from analogue to digital and introducing fleet-wide enhancements to terrain and attack radar systems to put the F-111 back on top of the league tables and keep it there for many years to come.

This photo album is a prelude to the full-length illustrated version due to be published by Arms & Armour Press in a few months, and so the contents of this project are aimed primarily at the modeller and those who desire a preparatory, pictorial glance at this pioneering machine. The photographs form the core of this work and to that end I am sincerely indebted to Frank B. Mormillo and those other ace photographers who went to so much trouble to contribute their work: my colleagues Peter E. Davies and David Robinson, Ben Knowles, and Tim Laming; also to the generosity of the USAF, General Dynamics, Grumman and Hughes for providing top quality material and letting cameras 'on base', especially Sergeant Deborah Aragon, Lieutenant-Colonel Donald Black, Kearney Bothwell, Virnell A. Bruce, SSgt Annette Crawford, Captain Alan C. Gregory, Peter E. Kirkup, Lois Lovisolo, SSgt Dave Malakoff, Captain Mary-Ann Neri, MSgt Stephen Pivnick, Fran Slimmer, Z. 'Joe' Thornton, Vincent Vinci, and Lieutenant-Colonel Joseph Wagovich; and to the Director of Arms & Armour Press, Rod Dymott, for his considerable help. Finally, special thanks to dedicated Crew Chief SSgt Ismael Sarraga, for letting me touch and photograph his 'baby': F-111E Zero-Seven-Eight, also known as 'Whispering Death', – *the* name for the 'Aardvark'.

▼ 3

3. The fourth General Dynamics F-111A, 63-9769, was the first example configured with movable pylons, synchronized with the variable-geometry (swing) wings. It was used as an aerodynamic testbed by the USAF Air Force Flight Test Center (AFFTC) at Edwards AFB, California, including spin-recovery and stores compatibility trials. Apart from the white nose and matt black anti-dazzle panel this aircraft was left in natural metal finish. Note the nose-up attitude of this lightly-loaded machine. (USAF)

4. On a test flight from General Dynamics Fort Worth, Texas, F-111A 63-9770 displays the Navy-style light gull grey and white decor common to early One-Elevens not left in natural metal finish. The swing-wings are being swept back from their full-forward setting of 16° as the machine picks up speed and pulls away from the chase aircraft. (General Dynamics)

5. Pre-flighting in progress in one of the voluminous Fort Worth hangars. The dual-hatch, sideways-opening cockpit canopy arrangement is unique to the F-111 series, and lends the machine its Aardvark appearance when viewed head-on. The early pre-production aircraft carried extensive test equipment, hence the highly instrumented nose probe and large number of technicians preening their charge. (General Dynamics)

▲ 6

6. The all-metal finish F-111A 63-9769, displaying flaps and wing root rotating gloves to good effect. Also just visible is the spin-recovery parachute canister mounted near the jetpipes, and dummy Phoenix missiles and pylons fashioned from glassfibre. The dark strip blended into the fin is the HF shunt antenna. (General Dynamics)

7. Close-up of the tail of the very first F-111A, 63-9766. Of particular interest are the pointed 'speed bumps' on each side of the powerplants, later replaced by blunt fairings incorporating AN/ALQ-94 ECM receivers and transmitters, and the fuel vent pipe between the exhaust nozzles. The first F-111A flight was made on 21 December 1964 with GD test pilot Dick Johnson at the helm. (General Dynamics)

▼ 7

8, 9. Under the TFX-N (Navy) programme, five prototype and two production F-111Bs were built by the major subcontractor Grumman. Attack and terrain following radar (TFR) systems were replaced by Hughes' AWG-9 fire control system, dedicated to fleet defence. BuNo 151971, the second testbed, displays its variable-geometry wings at their fully-swept 72.5° setting. Compared to the 'A' model, the 'B's wings were extended by 3.5 feet each and the nose shortened by 6.75 feet, the better to accommodate operations from the US Navy's carriers. The white tips to the elevons are for cosmetic purposes – each slab moves as a solid single unit. (Grumman)

10. BuNo 151974, the fifth and last F-111B prototype, displays full flaps and forward-swept wing during Grumman's Glide Scope (controllability) Program at Calverton, Long Island. Seven test pilots – five Navy, one Grumman and one from General Dynamics – made 216 passes on a simulated carrier deck which included a mirror 'meatball' landing aid, just like the real thing. The F-111B's tyres, optimized for carrier decks, were some 5 inches narrower and slighter in diameter than the chunky, lower-pressure 47x18in USAF versions. (Grumman)

8 ▲

9 ▲   10 ▼

EJECTABLE
CREW
MODULE

← RESCUE

CAUTION BOTH CANOPIES MUST BE LATCHED

▲11 ▼12

11. Grumman Chief Test Pilot Ralph 'Dixie' Donnell, and Dave Cook from the Government Flight Acceptance Department, in F-111B BuNo 151974's cockpit in November 1966. Like BuNo 151973, this aircraft incorporated the Super Weight Improvement Program reductions, taking the empty aircraft down to approximately 43,000lb; but the aircraft remained too heavy for safe carrier operations even after the follow-on Colossal Weight Improvement Programs. In addition to the temporary shiny metal finish, this aircraft is fitted with the radical 'escape and survival vehicle' (escape capsule), which replaced the conventional ejection seats seen in photograph 13. All F-111s starting with the fourth 'B' and twelfth 'A' were so equipped. Ralph Donnell flew the F-111B's maiden flight on 18 May 1965, in BuNo 151970. (Grumman)

12. F-111B pilot's view of his left console. Scanning clockwise, the throttles, sliding swing-sweep handle (near the canopy sill), landing gear lever, primary flight control instruments and control column are in view. The hand-held megaphone near the pilot's bucket seat was used to pass messages (or other suitable commentary) to the ground technicians over the din of the aircraft's engines. This means of communication is not used at an operational level: a plug-in lead which gives the aircraft's Captain or Crew Chief access to the flyer's intercom system is employed instead. (Hughes)

13. F-111B BuNo 151972's cockpit with AWG-9 fire control system displays and controls in view. Note the extensive data link, ADF and communications controls in the centre of the dashboard, and the Douglas Escapac seats. (Hughes)

14. Aerodynamic repre-sentations of the Hughes XAIM-54 Phoenix are put through their paces on F-111B testbed BuNo 151973. The infra-red search and track sensor protrudes from under the nose and the black-and-white steel arresting hook is shown to good advantage under the tail. Air Force F-111s have a hook also, for BAK (runway emergency aid) use, but it is largely concealed. (Grumman)

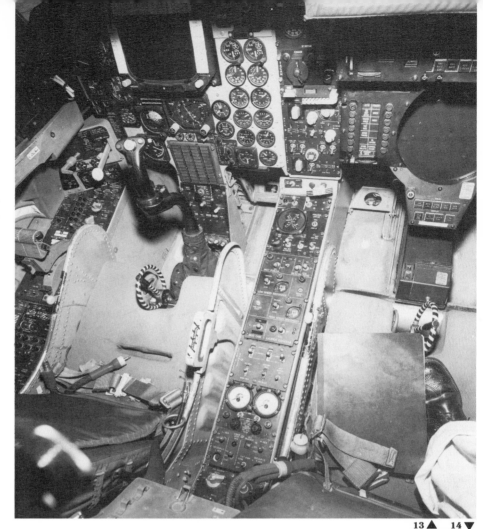

13 ▲   14 ▼

▲ 15

15. XAIM-54 Phoenix test round on BuNo 152715. Note also the revised Triple Plow intake configuration with its double blow-in doors (replaced by three doors on later USAF aircraft) which superseded the translating cowl design. (Hughes)

16. F-111B BuNo 151972 was one of four aircraft bailed to Hughes Aircraft Company to perform integration trials with the AWG-9/AIM-54 weapons system. The F-111B programme was cancelled in May 1968 but tests continued so that the valuable air-to-air package could be fine-tuned in good time for the follow-on Grumman VFX F-14A Tomcat effort. Tragically, two of the F-111Bs bailed to Hughes were lost during the course of radar and missile trials in 1968–9, taking two Hughes flight test people with them. (Hughes)

▲ 16   ▼ 17

17. The USAF's first combat deployment to South East Asia with the One-Eleven was in March 1968 as Project 'Combat Lancer', under the command of Colonel 'Ike' Dethman. In this photograph, taken at Takhli RTAB, Thailand, on 26 March 1968, the 'Combat Lancer' team line up in front of one of the six special 'Harvest Reaper' F-111As. From left to right, front row: Tom Germschied, Joe Hodges, Ike Dethman, Dean Salimer, Ed Palmgren, Bruce Ashley (USN) and Roger Nunnamaker. Rear: Mac Armstrong, Charlie Arnet, Rick Matteis, Joe Keene, Les Holland, Sandy Marquardt, Bill Coltman, Hank McGann, Bill Sealy, Dennis Graham, Spade Cooley (USN), Ken Powell, Norm Rice and Charlie Tosten. (Via Rick Matteis)

18. During the 474th TFW's second combat deployment to Takhli in 1972, some 48 F-111As from the 429th and 430th TFSs flew an average of 20–24 sorties a day, increasing to 33 a day at the height of the Christmas 1972 Linebacker II campaign. Here, a 429th 'Black Falcons' F-111A takes on fuel ('conducts AAR') from a KC-135A during Operation 'Constant Guard V', the twin-staged deployment to SEA. Crews complained that the tanker people hadn't been properly briefed, and that rendezvous had to be made at unfamiliar and varied altitudes. Other niggles were confronted, but the units involved 'tarted-up' the base at Takhli and the runway, revetments and other facilities were 'spruced-up' in good time for the fearsome Linebacker II initiative. (USAF)

19. F-111A taxiing and displaying full flaps and spoilers. The high rate of knots achieved during low-level flight has worn away the paint from the leading edges of the wings. (Frank B. Mormillo)

20. Whoops! A 474th TFW crew experiencing an uneasy moment during touchdown; perhaps a one-wheel landing, but more likely the result of strong crosswinds. F-111s have a 35-knot crosswind limit. (Frank B. Mormillo)

18 ▲

19 ▲   20 ▼

21. F-111A 67-0057 on the apron at Nellis AFB, Nevada. Note the elevons in typical parked, nose-down control posture, and the wings swept back fully at 72.5°. Aircraft are usually parked with the wings set at 16° to facilitate stores loading, while some 80 per cent of One-Eleven maintenance and pre- and post-sortie inspections require that the wings be extended. (Frank B. Mormillo)

22. Bicentennial F-111A 67-0076, the flagship of the 474th TFW. Standard crew boarding ladders lie near the nosewheel. (Don Logan via Ben Knowles)

23. F-111A 67-065 taxies at Nellis with SUU-20 practice dispenser on the wing pylons, and AN/ALQ-87 noise jamming electronic countermeasures (ECM) pod on one of the ventral hardpoints used only for ECM or data-link equipment. The

▲ 21   ▼ 22

training dispenser is used to carry rockets and up to six 25lb BDU-33 low drag or Mk106 high drag practice bombs. (Frank B. Mormillo)

24. Beautiful close-up shot of the General Electric, electrically driven M61A-1 20mm 'Gatling' gun, including its 2,084-round drum. Here it equips a Nellis-based F-111A, though nowadays it is used as standard equipment only on the F-111D; the starboard hinged bomb bay door assembly is removed and the entire gunpack hoisted into place, bolted in, and wired up. Other USAF models have the capability, but do not use the system in practice, keeping the bay clear for additional fuel tanks, nuclear weapons, or the Pave Tack targeting system. An AN/ALQ-87 ECM pod is shown to good advantage too. (Frank B. Mormillo)

▲ 25

▲ 26   ▼ 27

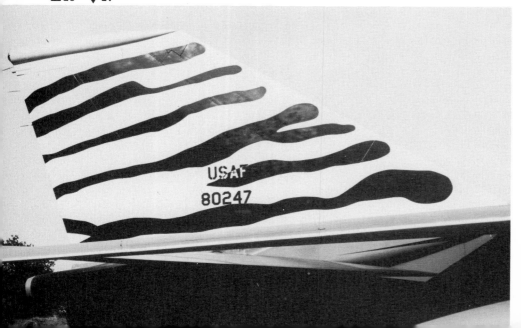

25. A feature common to all One-Elevens is the ability to 'make like a rocket', by jettisoning fuel through the aft vent and setting it alight via the hot exhaust. This dumping feature might be used in a 'fire-in-face' mode to protect the aircraft from a trailing interceptor or missile; 'bomb-in-face' techniques *are* briefed. This FB-111A demonstrates the torching technique to an excited audience at Edwards AFB in 1973. (Frank B. Mormillo)

26. Although SAC's 'heavies' fly 'Red Flag' or 'Green Flag' missions directly from their home bases, 8th Air Force FB-111As usually deploy to Nellis for the exercises, along with their entourage of maintenance and support personnel. 69-6513, depicted here tucking up its sturdy gear on take-off, was the penultimate FB-111A built. (Frank B. Mormillo)

27. FB-111A 68-0247 from the 393rd Bomb Squadron, 509th 'Enola Gay' Bomb Wing, wore this impressive black-and-yellow tail for the 1978 NATO 'Tiger Meet'. The remainder of the airframe was in standard SAC three-tone camouflage with white undersides and blue star-spangled band on the nose. (MAP)

28. Ground ordnance technicians from the 380th Munitions Maintenance Squadron (MMS) secure a concrete-filled nuclear 'training shape' on to a Plattsburgh-based One-Eleven. SAC's FB-111A fleet fly the strategic nuclear mission using free-fall, parachute-retarded gravity bombs and AGM-69 Short Range Attack Missiles, used also to smack radar defences *en route* to the primary target. Several FB-111A navigator-bombardiers are electronic warfare specialists and wear the 'Swing Wing Crow Defendere' patch. (USAF)

29. 509th MMS personnel perform weapons loading. The black scoop-shaped manipulator arm ensures safe cradling of the heavy nuclear bombs and casings. A quad castor-wheel fitting is used to lug conventional bombs. (USAF)

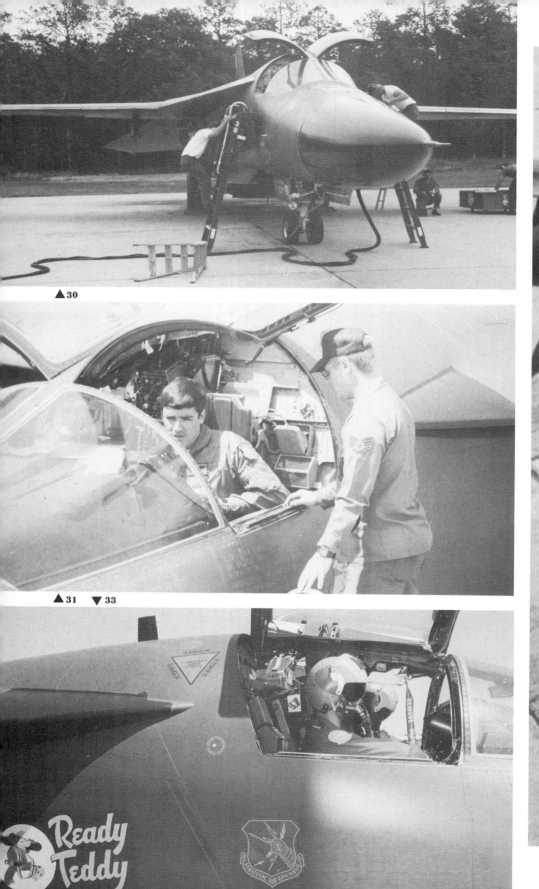

▲30

▲31 ▼33

30. Pre-flighting a 380th BW FB-111A in progress. A mission tape is 'fed' into the bird's MKIIB avionics system, containing all the information on the pre-planned route waypoints, target and multiple offset aimpoints. The right-hand seater then calls them up by punching the appropriate buttons on the navigation and attack panel. (USAF)

31. 68-0245's Crew Chief exchanges a few words with a 529th BS crew flying 'Ready Teddy'. The pilot and navigator undertake extensive pre-flight checks prior to launch. (USAF)

32. With crew on board, an FB-111A from the 380th Bomb Wing based at Plattsburgh AFB, New York is ready to start up and roll. The black rectangle on the nose hides the automatic direction finder (ADF) antenna; the circular glass optical component is the astro-tracker, a similar system to that employed in the SR-71 Habu. The machine wears the smart new dark-grey and green decor. (USAF)

33. 'Ready Teddy' artwork on a Plattsburgh-based FB-111A, serial 68-0245. The brown bear means business, carrying bomb and machine-gun, though the bomber it is painted on is not equipped with guns, using its bomb bay for additional fuel tanks or nuclear weapons instead. (USAF)

34. Viewed from a KC-10A Extender, a 380th BW FB-111A takes on fuel via the flying boom while another bomber lurks below. SAC's comparatively petite FB-111As rely heavily upon aerial refuelling and so the technique is practised frequently. (USAF photograph by MSgt Buster Kellum)

▲ 32

34 ▼

35. Dominating the navigator's control panels in the RAAF RF-111C is the radar display and hood. To the top left are the TFR scope and threat warning indicator; below those is the CRT display used in conjunction with the RF-111C's TV viewfinder equipment. F-111C/D/Fs have a similar electro-optic viewing capability, made possible by the F-111C/F's Pave Tack 'VID' and F-111D's 'AVE-TV' and 'Weapon TV' functions. Forward of the control stick –

all marks with the exception of the F-111B and EF-111A are dual-control – are the main navigation and attack controls, with recon and armament selection controls on the right-hand console. The layout is very similar to that of the F-111A/E models. (RAAF)

36. F-111C 'T-F'ing' over Australia with full thrust engaged and an impressive load of twenty-four Mk82 low-drag bombs. No tactical aircraft,

including Fencer and Tornado, can match the Aardvark's ordnance capacity without severely degrading speed or endurance. (RAAF)

37. RF-111C A8-126 with recce installation visible in the bomb bay. RAAF RF-111Cs retain full bomb-release capability in 'step' and 'train' release sequences using the Mk I analogue 'nav & attack' system, though all stores must be mounted on the wings. (General Dynamics)

38. This white-bellied F-111C, A8-132, serves with the RAAF's special Air Research Development Unit (ARDU) at Edinburgh, South Australia, performing trials with weapons systems and avionics. Note the calibration markings and the black-and-white Texas Instruments Paveway II GBU-10 laser-guided bombs. The ARDU badge is black and yellow and the rear of the fin cap is painted orange. (RAAF/Australian DoD)

36 ▲

37 ▲   38 ▼

EVOLUTION

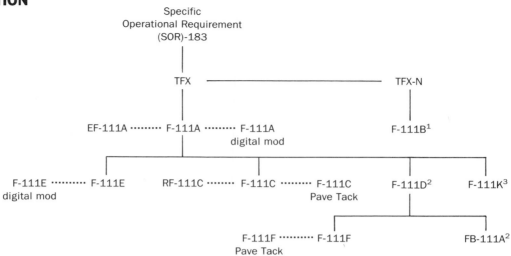

.... Conversion   ——— Follow-on model.
1. Production programme of 231 aircraft cancelled after 7 built.
2. Proposals to convert the aircraft to FB-111B/C or FB-111H standard not proceeded with.
3. Production programme of 50 aircraft cancelled after 2 prototypes nearly completed; aircraft on the assembly lines were subsequently built to FB-111A standard for the USAF.

OPERATIONAL UNITS

Squadron	Wing	Base, Location and Command	Type	Tailcode	Sqn Colour
389th TFTS 391st TFS	366th TFW	Mountain Home AFB, Idaho. 12th Air Force (AF), Tactical Air Command (TAC), USAF.	F-111A	MO	Yellow Blue
390th ECS	366th TFW	Mountain Home AFB, Idaho. 12th AF, TAC, USAF.	EF-111A	MO	(Red)
528th BS 529th BS 530th CCTS	380th BW	Plattsburgh AFB, New York. 8th AF, Strategic Air Command (SAC), USAF.	FB-111A	—	
393rd BS 715th BS	509th BW	Pease AFB, New Hampshire. 2nd AF, SAC, USAF.	FB-111A	—	
No. 1 Sqn	82nd SW	RAAF Amberley, Queensland, Australia. RAAF.	F-111C	—	Yellow
No. 6 Sqn	82nd SW	RAAF Amberley, Queensland, Australia. RAAF.	RF/F-111A/C	—	Blue
522nd TFS 523rd TFS 524th TFTS	27th TFW	Cannon AFB, New Mexico. 12th AF, TAC, USAF.	F-111D	CC	Red Blue Yellow
55th TFS 77th TFS 79th TFS	20th TFW	RAF Upper Heyford, England. 3rd AF, USAFE.	F-111E	UH	Blue/white Red Tiger
42nd ECS	66th ECW	Sembach AB, West Germany. 17th AF, USAFE (Unit physically located at Upper Heyford).	EF-111A	UH	Grey
492nd TFS 493rd TFS 494th TFS 495th TFTS	48th TFW	RAF Lakenheath, England. 3rd AF, USAFE.	F-111F	LN	Blue Yellow Red Green

BS/W	Bomb Squadron/Wing	ECS/W	Electronic Combat Squadron/Wing	TFS/W	Tactical Fighter Squadron/Wing
CCTS	Combat Crew Training Squadron	SW	Strike Wing	TFTS	Tactical Fighter Training Squadron

SPECIFICATIONS

	F-111A	EF-111A	FB-111A	F-111B	F-111C	F-111D	F-111E	F-111F
Mainplane wingspan								
@ 16°	63ft	63ft	70ft	70ft	70ft	63ft	63ft	63ft
@ 72.5°	31ft 11in	31ft 11in	33ft 11in	33ft 11in	33ft 11in	31ft 11in	31ft 11in	31ft 11in
Horizontal tail span	29ft 4in	29ft 4in	29ft 4in	29ft 4in	29ft 4in	29ft 4in	29ft 4in	29ft 4in
Length	73ft 6in	74ft	73ft 6in	66ft 9in	73ft 6in	73ft 6in	73ft 6in	73ft 6in
Height	17ft 1in	20ft	17ft 1in	15ft 9in	17ft 1in	17ft 1in	17ft 1in	17ft 1in
Maximum takeoff weight (approx.)	91,300lb	89,000lb	114,300lb	79,000lb	114,300lb	100,000lb	91,000lb	100,000lb
Power plant (×2)	TF30-P-3	TF30-P-3	TF30-P-7	TF30-P-12	TF30-P-3	TF30-P-9	TF30-P-3	TF30-P-100
Takeoff thrust	37,000lb st	37,000lb st	40,700lb st	40,500lb st	37,000lb st	41,680lb st	37,000lb st	50,200lb st
Mission avionics	Mk I NAS	TJS	Mk IIB/ Astro NAS	AWG-9	Mk I NAS	Mk II NAS	Mk I NAS	Mk IIB NAS
Unique capabilities	–	TJS	AGM-69 SRAM	AIM-54 Phoenix	AGM-84 Harpoon AVQ-26 Pave Tack	Interactive displays	–	GBU-15 AVQ-26 Pave Tack
Triple Plow inlets: translating cowls (TC) or blow-in (BI)	TC	TC	No. 1 TC No. 2+ BI	Nos. 1-6 TC No. 7 BI	TC	BI	BI	Bi
Notes	Early aircraft fitted with TF30-P-1 engines. Only aircraft No. 31 onward deployed to combat units.	Aircraft undergoing upgrade to TJS and are receiving TF30-P-9 engines.	First model to receive the updated AN/ALQ-137 deception jammer and AN/ALR-62 threat-warning upgrade.	Includes five prototypes, powered by TF30-P-1.	Four later adapted to the RF-111C reconnaissance configuration.	–	First model to achieve IOC at full unit strength.	Saw action in the 1986 Libya raid. First type to receive Pave Tack pod.
Numbers built	159	42	76	7	24	96	94	106

SERIAL NUMBERS

F-111A
AF 63-9766 to -9783	18
AF 65-5701 to -5710	10
AF 66-0011 to -0058	48
AF 67-0032 to -0114	83

F-111B
BuNo 151970 to 151974	5
BuNo 152714 & 151715	2

F-111C
RAAF 67-0125 to -0148	24

F-111D
AF 68-0085 to -0180	96

F-111E
AF 67-0115 to -0124	10
AF 68-0001 to -0084	84

F-111F
AF 70-2362 to -2419	58
AF 71-0883 to -0894	12
AF 72-1441 to -1452	12
AF 73-0707 to -0718	12
AF 74-0177 to -0188	12

FB-111A
AF 67-0159 to -0163	5
AF 67-7192 to -7196	5

AF 68-0239 to -0292	54
AF 69-6503 to -6514	12

EF-111A
AF 66-0013 to -0016	4
AF 66-0018 to -0021	4
AF 66-0023	1
AF 66-0027 & -0028	2
AF 66-0030 & -0031	2
AF 66-0033	1
AF 66-0035 to -0039	5
AF 66-0041	1
AF 66-0044	1
AF 66-0046 to -0051	6

AF 66-0055 to -0057	3
AF 67-0032 to -0035	4
AF 67-0037 to -0039	3
AF 67-0041 & -0042	2
AF 67-0044	1
AF 67-0048	1
AF 67-0052	1

Aircraft serials are painted on the vertical stabilizer in abbreviated form; e.g., F-111F AF 74-0178 appears as AF72-178. RAAF aircraft use a different form; e.g., F-111C 67-0147 appears as A8-147. Three-digit serials appear on the nosegear doors; e.g., F-111E 68-0078 appears as 078. This is true for all aircraft except the EF-111A, which often has the fiscal-year number and last two digits; e.g., EF-111A 67-0035 appears as 735.

FB-111A 67-0160, the second production example, in gull grey and white decor. The intakes on this aircraft featured two blow-in doors, whereas all subsequent FB-111As were equipped with three. 67-0160 served with the Edwards AFFTC test organization until it was retired to the desert 'boneyard' at Davis-Monthan AFB, Arizona, in 1974, by which time it had lost the SAC band and markings near the cockpit and had adopted a matt-black radome. It has since been 'butchered' for spares.

F-111E 68-0078, nicknamed 'Whispering Death', depicted in April 1988 when serving with the 77th TFS, 20th TFW, at RAF Upper Heyford, USAFE. The nose art is shown to good advantage in photo 74, and other close-ups of Zero-Seven-Eight appear in photos 70 and 75–8 inclusive. The fin cap is bright red and the wheel hubs white, with red centre nuts. Serial number and four-line legend on the port nosegear door is in white and reads: ACFT COMMANDER, CAPT CROWELL, DEDICATED CREWCHIEF, SSGT SARRAGA. The starboard nosegear door is similarly painted, but bears the five-line legend: WEAPONS SYS OFFICER, CAPT SANDS, ASST DEDICATED CREWCHIEF, A1C ROSS, SPECIALIST A1C CANT. National insignia are in red, white and blue, and the starboard side bears the 20th TFW emblem in full colour. The camouflage scheme consists of the standard Vietnam night colours.

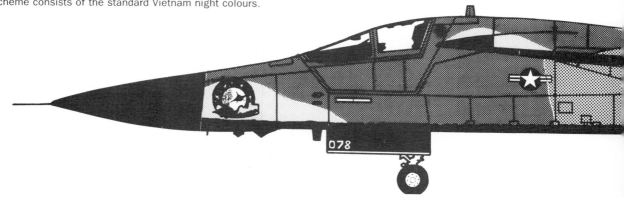

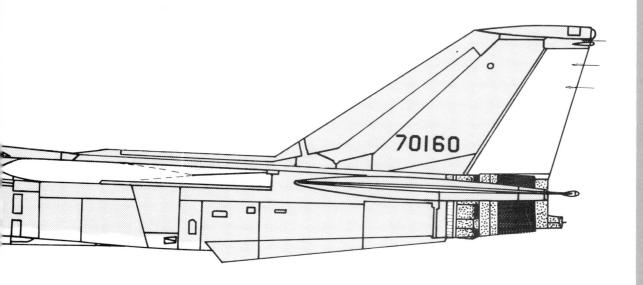

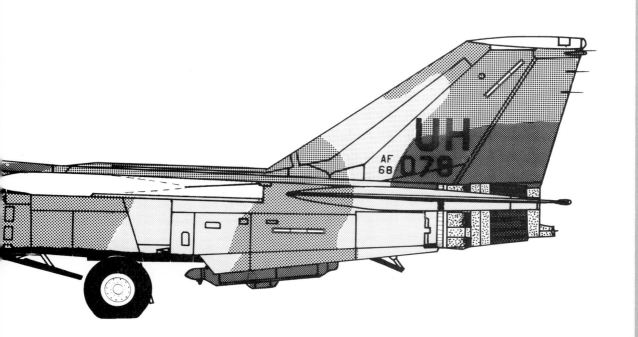

F-111 AARDVARK

CONVENTIONAL WEAPONS

Bombs — old range

Mk 82 Low-drag 'slick'	500lb Freefall.
Mk 82 High-drag Snakeye	500lb Freefall, airbrake-fin retarded.
Mk 84 Low-drag 'slick'	2,000lb Freefall.
CBU-58 Cluster-bomb unit	750lb Freefall, dispensing.

Weapons — new range

Mk 82 AIR Ballute	500lb ⎫ Freefall, with optional
Mk 84 AIR Ballute	2,000lb ⎬ low-drag, or high-drag air-inflatable retard facility.
BLU-107 Durandal	(all-up) 430lb Rocket-assisted anti-runway, with parachute retard.
CBU-87 Combined Effects Munitions	950lb Freefall; 202 various effect sub-munitions.
Gator Air-Delivered Mine	500lb Freefall; 94 anti-armour/ anti-personnel mines.
GBU-10 Paveway II	2,000lb Freefall glide; Mk 84-adapted, laser-guided.
GBU-15 Wide-chord cruciform	2,000lb Freefall glide; Mk 84-adapted, TV- or imaging infra-red guided.
GBU-24 Paveway III	2,000lb Freefall flown; Mk 84-adapted, low-level laser-guided bomb (LLLGB).
AGM-84A Harpoon	(all-up) 1,160lb Stand-off anti-ship missile.
AIM-9P Sidewinder	(all-up) 172lb Infra-red-guided air-to-air missile. Lima and Mike models will soon replace the Papa version, an upgraded AIM-9E/J.

Nuclear Weapons

B-61	(all-up) 708lb Primary tactical nuclear weapon of F-111E/Fs standing on 'Victor Alert'; also used by FB-111As. Comes in different versions; parachute retarded.
Tiger B-61	(classified) Rocket-assisted version of the B-61, believed to be entering production.
B-83	(classified) Latest nuclear round.
AGM-69 SRAM I	(all-up) 2,230lb Stand-off nuclear missile used by FB-111As, with Radiating Site Target Acquisition system.

These represent the most commonly employed weapons systems. The GBU-15 is now entering the inventory in short-chord versions, which are cheaper to produce and which are compatible with SUU-54-class, 2000lb cluster-bombs. A rocket-assisted version, known as the AGM-130, outwardly similar to the short-chord GBU-15 but with a rocket booster strapped to the casing, is undergoing tests at Eglin Armament Development Test Center, Florida. Millimetre-wave-(MMW)-guided, autonomous target-searching models of the GBU-24 or GBU-15 may soon be available.

COLOUR SCHEMES

Intakes, bomb-bay interior, gear legs and wheel wells are white, but areas exposed by deployed flaps and spoilers, including the interiors of the control surfaces and maingear 'barn door', are red. Wheel hubs are either white or a bright metal colour, with hub nuts often painted in the squadron colour. Tyres are distinctly black.

The basic cockpit colour is a medium grey, with black instruments and matt-black forward coaming, canopy sills and cockpit framing. Seat cushions are olive-green, seat-belts a dark olive-brown, and headrests bright red.

The interior of the F-111 airframe, accessed by maintenance panels, is zinc-chromate coloured, with black avionics boxes. Pale-lemon electro-luminescent formation strip-lights, a recent retrofit, are located on the fuselage, fin and near the wing carry-through box. Engine nozzles and the large structure containing the fuel dump outlet between them are left in natural metal. Wing 'boots' (the slot covers) are olive-drab.

Practice dispensers were painted white, as were AN/ALQ-87 ECM pods. Later AN/ALQ-119 ECM pods were painted black. The new AN/ALQ-131 ECM pod is painted medium olive-green, as is the Pave Tack pod, AN/AXQ-14 data-link pod and all practice munitions dispensers. Inert ordnance, including BDU-33 practice bombs, are predominantly blue; Mk 106 practice bombs are bright orange. Live ordnance is painted dark green, with a yellow band near the nose. GBU-15 advanced electro-optic munitions are based on standard dark green Mk 84s or cluster-munitions, but have nose and tail attachments that appear bronze coloured. Nuclear training rounds are white, but most live versions, such as the B-61, are left in natural metal finish. The AGM-69 SRAM is white, regardless of configuration. F-111 wing pylons are painted in sympathy with the aircraft's under-surface colour — i.e., black, white or pale grey.

In the schemes detailed below, five-digit codes refer to Federal Standards (FS) 595a numbers.

Navy Scheme — early F-111A, FB-111A, and F-111B

Gull grey	36440	upper surfaces.
White	17875	undersides and control surfaces.

Service logos were in black, with full red, white and blue national insignia. Stencil data consisted of black, red and yellow markings, and black 'walkway' lines. USAF nose radomes were cream.

Vietnam Night Scheme – F-111A/C/D/E/F and RF-111C

Dark green	34079	
Medium green	34102	upper surfaces.
Tan brown	30219	
Black	—	under surfaces.

Early camouflaged examples wore white undersides, while 'Combat Lancer' F-111As had 34079 dark-green under-surfaces. Stencil data colours varied over the years; originally they were the same colours as the Navy scheme but with yellow data on the black undersides. Later the data on the upper surfaces was sprayed on in a contrasting camouflage colour – e.g., green data on tan camouflage and vice-versa, with some red and black data retained. Tail codes and serial numbers were in white, but since 1979 they have been applied in black. Full colour, but miniature national insignia have largely been replaced by low-visibility black markings on the USAF aircraft.

Strategic Scheme – FB-111A

Dark green	34079	
Blue-green	34159	upper surfaces.
Tan-green	34201	
White	37875	under surfaces.

Stencil data was similar to the Vietnam night camouflage but with black stencil data on the under-surfaces. National insignia were full colour, in miniature, and the serial number was applied to the fin in a contrasting camouflage colour.

Strategic Lizard Scheme – FB-111A

Dark grey	34091	
Dark green	34096	overall.

The Lizard scheme started to replace the old Strategic scheme from about 1986. Some red stencil data is retained, but the majority is in black, as is the national insignia. The tail serial is applied in a contrasting camouflage colour.

Ghost Grey – EF-111A

Medium grey	36320	upper surfaces.
Pale grey	36492	flanks of fuselage, nose radome and under surfaces.
Insignia grey	36231	USAF logos and national insignia.

Stencil data is in Insignia grey and red.

MODEL KITS CURRENTLY AVAILABLE

1/72nd scale kits

Airfix	F-111E	
Esci	F-111A	
Esci	EF-111A	Due for release in 1988
Hasegawa	FB-111A	
Monogram	EF-111A	

1/48th scale kits

Academy/ Minicraft	F-111A	
Minicraft	EF-111A	
Minicraft	FB-111A	Due for release in 1988
Minicraft	F-111C	
Minicraft	F-111F	
Monogram	F-111A	

Decals

Microscale 72-132 – Markings for a development F-111A (see photos 3–7), Combat Lancer era F-111A, 474th TFW F-111A (see photos 21 and 23), F-111B Phoenix testbed (see photos 13 and 16), FB-111A with 2nd Air Force badge, F-111C, and 20th TFW F-111E are included.

Microscale 72-450 – Markings are included for FB-111A 68-0247 in 'Tiger Meet' scheme (see photo 27), FB-111A 68-0269 nicknamed the 'New Hampshire Special', and F-111E 68-0020 in Bicentennial decor.

Microscale 72-451 – Markings are included for two EF-111As: 66-049 in overall red, white and blue decor, and 66-018 from the 390th ECS, 366th TFW, in subdued two-tone grey (see photo 51).

Microscale 72-452 – Complete stencil data for two F-111s. Early black and red type data.

Microscale 72-512 – Includes markings for FB-111A 67-0159 in overall white with red trim, and F-111F 70-2376 with Bicentennial markings (see photo 39).

Microscale 72-542 – Two F-111Es and one F-111F are included: E 68-020 nicknamed 'My Lucky Blonde' (see photo 64), E 68-077 nicknamed 'June Nite' and F 72-448 nicknamed 'Miss Liberty' (see photos 86 and 87).

Microscale 48-228 – As 72-450 but without the Bicentennial F-111E.

Microscale 48-229 – F-111 stencil data for one aircraft. Early black and red type data.

Microscale 48-250 – Two Bicentennial F-111s: E 68-0020 from the 20th TFW and F 70-2376 from the 366th TFW (see photo 39).

Microscale 48-315 – As 72-542.

Modeldecal No. 91 – Full 1/72nd scale markings for one of 13 EF-111As based at Upper Heyford with the 42nd ECS as of 31 July 1987, all with nose art (see photos 56–8).

▲ 39

▲ 40 ▼ 41

39. F-111Fs were assigned originally to the 347th TFW, later redesignated 366th TFW, at Mountain Home AFB, Idaho. In Bicentennial Year 70-2376 wore this flamboyant trim while the CO's jet, 70-2366, wore a slightly more subdued version which featured all the Wing's squadron insignia. (Map)

40. The 366th TFW took over Nellis's F-111As in 1977 and transferred its F-111Fs to the 48th TFW at Lakenheath, USAFE, as part of Operation 'Ready Switch'. This 'A' model has its 'barn door' airbrake open (the last operation in the undercarriage retraction sequence, but an in-flight option) as it departs Nellis in December 1979 with eight Snakeye bombs. (Frank B. Mormillo)

41. Mountain Home-based F-111F tucks up its gear on take-off in 1976. The 366th TFW made an emergency deployment to Teagu AB, South Korea that year when the North accused the USA of violating the neutral zone. Tensions ran high and the presence of the F-111Fs helped cool things down considerably! (Frank B. Mormillo)

42. 366th TFW F-111A equipped with gunpack, practice bomb dispenser plus Bomb Release Units (BRUs), in the landing pattern around Nellis. Note the area of flap that has been replaced and which retains its primer undercoat. Major strip and respray is performed once every eight years, with major touch-up work performed at depot-level every 48 months. Minor and decorative touch-up work is done on base by the Crew Chief or one of his or her colleagues. (Frank B. Mormillo)

43. Bombs away: a salvo of 24 'slick' Mk 82 inert 500lb bombs leaves F-111A 67-061 during a training mission. USAF One-Eleven crews are provided with the necessary resources (munitions *and* range time) to expend considerably quantities of ordnance – the one advantage of being classed a 'bomber'. Delivery techniques available include angular, level, low-angle drogue, toss, and loft, employing one or more of a combination of visual or radar in automatic or manual modes. The options are considerable. (USAF)

▲ 44

▲ 45   ▼ 46

44. F-111E 67-0120 from the 57th FWW complete with Westinghouse AN/ALQ-119 ECM pod (just visible between the strakes), at Nellis AFB in 1971. Today, Nellis's five 431st Test & Evaluation Squadron, 57th FWW One-Elevens are detached to McClellan AFB, California. F-111E 67-0120 is now nicknamed 'The Chief' and operates with the 20th TFW at Upper-Heyford, England (see photographs 72 & 73). (Westinghouse)

45. The fifth F-111D, 68-089, decorated in standard Vietnam night camouflage and special dots, at Edwards AFFTC in 1973. The 6512th Test Squadron continues to operate five One-Elevens, including an 'A', an 'E', and three 'Ds'.

46. AFFTC F-111A flies chase to a Rockwell B-1B in April 1985. The B-1B will oust the FB-111A from the strategic role once full operational capability has been achieved on the new swing-winger; the FB-111As will then be transferred to full-time tactical bombing with the new designation F-111G. (Frank B. Mormillo)

47. Displaying its large wings, F-111A 66-053 makes a low-level pass over Edwards. This aircraft served as testbed for the Grumman/Norden Pave Mover attack system but has since been demodified, as seen here. (Frank B. Mormillo)

47 ▲

48. The Eglin Armament Development Test Center & Tactical Air Warfare Center in Florida provides the necessary security for advanced munitions and electronic countermeasures development. Seen here is one of its three resident F-111Es, 68-058, equipped with rocket-assisted Rockwell International AGM-130 standoff electro-optic 'smart' bombs. These TV- or imaging infra-red-guided munitions are considerably more expensive than laser-guided bombs, but have the advantage that lock-on to target can be accomplished prior to launch (or after, using a data-link for standoff lock-on), permitting the crew to leave the target area after weapons release. (Rockwell International)

48 ▼

▲ 49

49. EF-111A 66-041 performed the lion's share of Phase I and 'CAT' testing at Calverton, and Eglin, Florida, for the Grumman/Eaton AN/ALQ-99E noise-jamming system; so much so that scheduled depot-level work had to be postponed – a rare thing. This fine photograph shows a Grumman test crew climbing in preparatory to a check hop from the Corporation's Calverton, Long Island facility in New York. (Grumman)

▼ 50

50. In addition to the fin cap, various antennae and ventral canoe mods designed to incorporate the AN/ALQ-99E Jamming Sub-System, related AN/ALQ-137 Self-Protection System and AN/ALR-62 Terminal Threat Warning System (collectively known as the Tactical Jamming System, or TJS), EF-111As underwent a complete overhaul while being reworked by Grumman. Of special interest here are the nose radars: the large parabolic dish of the AN/APQ-113 nav & attack radar, modified to AN/APQ-160 standard, and the two little antennae of the AN/APQ-110 TFR system. (Grumman)

51. Ghost-grey EF-111A Raven, 66-018, assigned to the 390th Electronic Combat Squadron (ECS), 366th TFW, at Mountain Home AFB, Idaho, Delivered by Grumman on 24 March 1983, it is seen here four months later while on deployment to Nellis during a 'Green Flag' electronic warfare exercise. (Frank B. Mormillo)

52. The CO's jet from the 390th ECS landing at Nellis in March 1986. It is one of only two Mountain Home aircraft – excluding the gate guardian, a demodified RF-111A testbed – to carry their standard 'Spirit of Idaho' nose art. Pioneering 390th ECS CO was Lieutenant Colonel Tom Pickering, who has considerable combat experience in the EB-66C and F-111A. The 366th TFW averages 8,000 sorties a year in its EF/F-111As. (Frank B. Mormillo)

53. Portside, static view of the CO's Raven 67-042 displaying its three tons of receiver and jamming modifications to good effect. 42 EF-111As were modified to the 'Spark 'Vark' configuration by Grumman, with all deliveries of operational aircraft taking place between November 1981 and December 1985, including the re-reworked testbeds.

51 ▲

52 ▲   53 ▼

▲ 54   ▼ 55

54. USAFE operates a dedicated radar-jamming unit, reactivated on 1 July 1983 under the command of Lieutenant Colonel Dave Vesely and subsequently equipped with Ravens also: the 42nd ECS, 66th ECW, headquartered at Sembach, West Germany, but based at RAF Upper-Heyford, England, alongside the 20th TFW's F-111Es so as to share One-Eleven maintenance resources. Here, 66-037 displays its medium-grey upper surfaces in a bank. Despite the heavy jamming equipment, which the EF-111A must carry *back home*

from the target, a combination of the early translating cowl intakes and recent switch to TF30-P-9 engines make the 'Spark' Vark' one of the fastest models. (Grumman)

55. Over-the-sill view of the EF-111A cockpit. The pilot's controls differ very little from those of the other F-111 variants – the 'D' model excluded – whereas the Electronic Warfare Officer's (EWO or 'Crow') office has been revised extensively. The large 10x8in screen provides details on jamming equipment status and hostile emissions being picked up, to help him 'manage' the largely automatic Tactical Jamming System. The 'Crow' 'talks' to the TJS via the pedestal control panel, which replaced the back-up control column. (Grumman)

56. 'Ye old Crow' artwork belonging to EF-111A 67-035 of the 42nd ECS, painted in insignia grey and pale lemon colours. The stencilled badge near the cockpit is that of the 66th ECW; compare that with the 20th TFW stencil applied to the 42nd ECS commander's aircraft in photograph 57. (David Robinson)

57. Close-up of the 'Let 'Em Eat Crow' artwork belonging to Raven 67-034, assigned to the commander of the 42nd ECS, Lieutenant Colonel Bill McAdams (now Lieutenant Colonel Roger W. Brooks). This clever legend blends the old expression which literally means to humble one's opponent by forcing him to eat raw crow with the professional name 'Crow' used by EWOs, past and present. The 'Old Crows' is one of the USAF's most prestigious 'clubs'. (Tim Laming)

58. 'Cherry Bomb', the nose art of EF-111A 67-052, was worn previously by an EB-66C in Vietnam. All of the 42nd ECS aircraft carried nose art from mid-1987 until April 1988, when orders came down the line to remove it all; some of the 42nd ECS' thirteen EF-111As have recently been replaced by fresh aircraft straight from the depot at McClellan, California.

56 ▲

57 ▲   58 ▼

▲59 ▼60

59. Described by One-Eleven drivers as 'cosmic', the Rockwell/Norden Mk II nav & attack system is used exclusively by the F-111D variant. Primary user is the 27th TFW based at Cannon AFB, New Mexico. (Frank B. Mormillo)

60. F-111D 68-137 from the 522nd TFS, 27th TFW, launching with eight live but 'dumb' Mk 82 500lb 'slicks'. All models can use 'smart' laser-guided weapons but autonomous target designation is available to the Pave Tack-equipped versions only. (General Dynamics)

61. With its exhaust cans glowing, F-111D 68-141 takes to the skies above Nellis armed with a pair of Mk 84 2,000lb bombs. Of the 96 'Ds' built, Cannon flies 72; an additional eight aircraft are engaged in test work. (Frank B. Mormillo)

62. 'Bombed-up' F-111Ds on the ramp at Cannon, out in the sun. By contrast, USAFE-based One-Elevens are all hidden away in protective TAB-V shelters. (Ben Knowles)

63. 'Red Flag', November 1984: Frank Mormillo's expert camera eye catches an impressive line-up of 27th TFW F-111Ds awaiting their next mission. The yellow F-111D badge near the radome is a feature of all Cannon's aircraft, as is the Wing badge near the cockpit. (Frank B. Mormillo)

61 ▲

62▲   63 ▼

▲ 64

▲ 65   ▼ 66

64. 'My Lucky Blonde', F-111E 68-0020 of the 20th TFW Commander in 1986. It has since flown out for depot-level work, and 'The Chief' has assumed the role of boss 'Vark' at Upper Heyford. 'My Lucky Blonde' artwork comprised black logo on a golden yellow scroll. (Tim Laming)

65. 77th TFS, 20th TFW F-111E on approach to RAF Upper Heyford in April 1988. The large area of flap provides substantial lift, and crews comment that the aircraft can continue flying even after touchdown, creating problems in strong crosswinds.

66. 20th TFW F-111E 68-0055, nicknamed 'Heartbreaker' and the official mount of the 55th TFS 'Blue Squadron' CO, Lieutenant Colonel Bill Savage. The colourful nose art on Upper Heyford's F-111Es has since been removed. (David Robinson)

67. 79th TFS 'Tigers' F-111E 68-0040 with the artwork 'The Other Woman'. Crew Chief SSgt Larry Casteel's wife thought up the name because of the amount of time her husband spent working on the aircraft. The artwork features a pink rose and green leaves, with yellow sign and black legend. Sadly, this and other artwork which decorated virtually every 20th TFW F-111E has since been removed. (David Robinson)

68. 'Red Lady II' adorned the nose of F-111E 68-0077, which also carried the legend '77th AMU' in bold black letters on its tail. This complex artwork comprised a mix of blues and reds and, like much of the 20th TFW's nose art, was applied to both sides of the aircraft. (David Robinson)

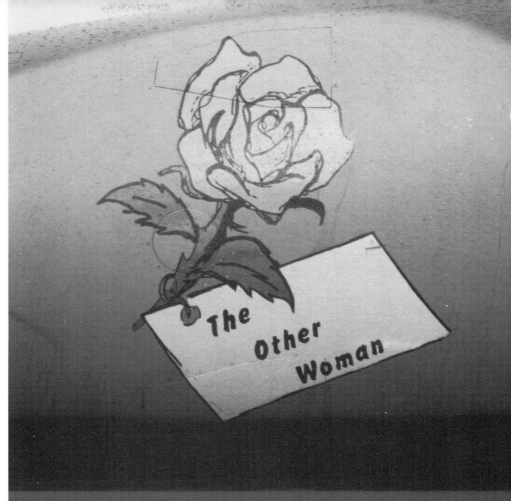

67 ▲ 68 ▼

▲ 69

69. 79th TFS F-111E 68-0073 overflying Nellis AFB with practice dispensers, BRUs, and short, two-band AN/ALQ-119 ECM pod installed. Because of the prolonged training programme undertaken by the 474th TFW at Nellis, and the grounding orders of the late 1960s, the 79th TFS actually was the first F-111 unit to achieve full operational capability, in 1970. The 79th TFS is presently commanded by Lieutenant Colonel Steven R. Emory and includes Captain Brad Insley in its ranks: Brad Insley is somewhat of an enigma in F-111 circles, with combat time on the type in South East Asia and more than 4,000 hours in the aircraft! (Frank B. Mormillo)

▼ 70

70. 77th TFS 'E' 68-0078
lurking in its TAB-V shelter at
Upper Heyford in April 1988.
The aircraft was nicknamed
'Whispering Death'. The 77th
TFS is commanded by
Lieutenant Colonel Jon G.
Safely; vice-commander is Dave
Skakal who, like many of his F-
111E colleagues, has
considerable prior experience in
the Phantom.

71. 'A Knight To Remember'
decorated both sides of 79th
TFS F-111E 68-0063's nose in
early 1988. The artwork
featured a white-and-blue
knight on a white horse, with
red bridle and grey shading, a
green dragon and blue legend,
superimposed on a yellow disc.
The nickname was inspired by a
local pub, the 'George and
Dragon!' The canopy framing
was in natural metal finish; the
large black knob-shaped device
under the artwork is part of the
F-111's recent AN/ALR-62 threat
warning kit upgrade, the other
protrusions comprising the
strike camera and UHF/Tacan
antenna. (Peter E. Davies)

72, 73. Assigned to 20th TFW,
Commander Colonel Graham
Shirley is F-111E 67-0120 seen
here taxiing to the take-off
runway at Upper Heyford. Nose
art, appropriately titled 'The
Chief', features a brown Red
Indian with black-and-white
head-dress, with the title logo in
red. Fin top colours, from front
to rear, represent the four One-
Eleven squadrons based in
Oxfordshire: yellow, blue, red
and grey. Note the divergent
posture of the exhaust feathers
in the close-up shot of the tail
area. (Peter E. Davies)

71 ▲

72 ▲   73 ▼

74. SSgt Sarraga's personal charge, F-111E 68-0078, nicknamed 'Whispering Death'; a name given to the One-Eleven originally by the Pathet Lao in the Plain des Jarres. Artwork comprises a black aircraft, trees and foreground, brick-red buildings, a pale pink centre roundel, and bright blue legend and outer roundel, the latter with white specks and crosses representing stars.

75. Close-up of the F-111's nosegear and capacious wheel well.

76. 'We use the biggest rubbers in the fighter community' was the jocular remark made by a Lakenheath pilot at the 1983 Greenham Common IAT. The whole assembly doubles up and retracts forward into the comparatively small wheel well '. . . as if by magic'.

▲ 74 ▼ 75 ▼ 76

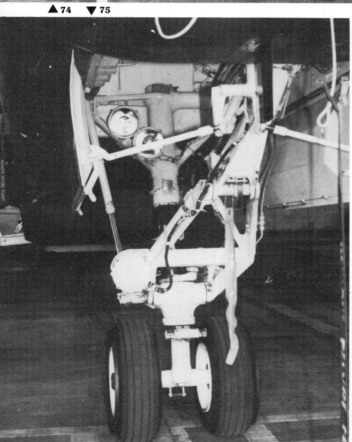

77. Side view of the starboard TF30-P-3 exhaust nozzle installed in 68-0078. Of special interest are the two rectangular holes, which dispense spring-loaded chaff & flare countermeasures cartridges.

78. An artform in itself: the complex five-stage augmented thrust nozzle of the Pratt & Whitney TF30-P-3 powerplant, rated at 18,500lb max. thrust with 'the can lit up'.

77▲   78▼

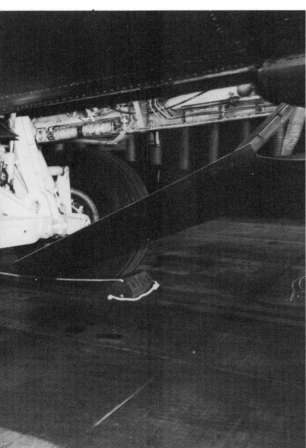

▲ 79

79. 48th TFW 'Statue of Liberty Wing' F-111F on approach at Nellis AFB after a 'Red Flag' sortie in November 1984. The aircraft is equipped with practice AIM-9E Sidewinder, BRUs, SUU-21 dispensers and

▼ 80

Pave Tack targeting pod. All four squadrons at Lakenheath have Pave Tack capability, the 494th TFS being the first operational unit to be equipped with the system. As well as marking targets for laser-guided

Paveway bombs, the laser gun can also be used to provide slant-range to the nav & attack computer to help compute the release of 'dumb', unguided bombs. 492nd TFS Wizzo Mike Conway pointed out that 'this

super capability is hard to practise in Europe because of restrictions on "squirting" the laser; Nellis is a definite plus in this respect'. (Frank B. Mormillo)

80. F-111F 71-0889 of the 493rd TFS, 48th TFW undergoing pre-flight work in one of Lakenheath's centrally located TAB-V shelters, used previously for the 'Victor Alert' mission. The aircraft is the responsibility of Crew Chief SSgt G. Gosa, and is nominally assigned to pilot Captain Don 'Title' Harrison and Wizzo Captain Tom 'Fingers' Lacombe. It is equipped with 600gal fuel tanks, Pave Tack, and dispensers loaded with Mk 106 practice bombs. (Peter E. Davies)

81. One of two F-111F testbeds that flew from McClellan AFB, California, as Pave Tack trials aircraft. The aircraft is also equipped with a wide-chord GBU-15 cruciform electro-optically-guided bomb and related AXQ-14 data-link pod for standoff communication with the weapon – now the speciality of the 493rd TFS at Lakenheath. One of the key figures in the Lakenheath GBU-15 programme was Major Dick Brown, now IP with the 495th 'Aardvark University' and runner-up to Brad Insley in the all-time high F-111 hours league, with more than 3,900 hours logged in the aircraft. (Ford Aerospace)

82. F-111F 70-2394 from 'Blue Squadron', the 492nd TFS, demonstrates aerodynamic and friction braking at Lakenheath in April 1988. The 492nd TFS is commanded by Lieutenant Colonel Tom Runge, who describes himself as an 'old codger' compared to his young colleagues. Tom Runge spent time at RAF Staff College where he presented a paper comparing the Tornado and F-111, drawing some interesting conclusions.

83. 492nd TFS F-111F takes to the sky on its TF30-P-100 powerplants, some 25-30 per cent more powerful than the other engines used in the F-111 series. The five-stage afterburner provides smooth transition to maximum power – no kick in the back. Note the 600 US gal drop tanks.

81▲

82▲   83▼

▲84 ▼85

86 ▲

87 ▲

84. 55th TFS, 20th TFW F-111E 68-074 drops four Mk 82 'slick' 500lb bombs while on a Weapons Training Deployment (WTD). 'Slick' and 'Snakeye' bombs have recently been replaced by a new, dual-mode bomb called the 'Ballute'. 'For the first time, we're getting weapons that were designed for the F-111,' commented Captain Greg Lowrimore, IWSO with the 77th TFS, 20th TFW. (General Dynamics/USAFE)

85. The One-Eleven community now has 'smart airplanes' *and* 'smart bombs': a 493rd TFS F-111F taxiing to the take-off runway with Pave Tack pod and Mk 84-adapted, 2,000lb Paveway II GBU-10 laser-guided bombs installed. Pave Tack and the GBU-10s were used with considerable success during the 'North Africa Bomb Competition' in April 1986. New Paveway III, low-level laser-guided bombs are entering the inventory, and will expand the delivery envelope to fast-and-

low. (Ford Aerospace via SSgt Dave Malakoff)

86, 87. F-111F 72-1448 nicknamed 'Miss Liberty', the flagship of the 48th TFW. Nose art is carried on the port side only, along with the wing badge; the starboard side features the badges of the 'Statue of Liberty Wing's' four squadrons.

The *Fotofax* series

A new range of pictorial studies of military subjects for the modeller, historian and enthusiast. Each title features a carefully-selected set of photographs plus a data section of facts and figures on the topic covered. With line drawings and detailed captioning, every volume represents a succinct and valuable study of the subject. New and forthcoming titles:

Warbirds
F-111 Aardvark
P-47 Thunderbolt
B-52 Stratofortress
Stuka!
Jaguar
US Strategic Air Power:
 Europe 1942–1945
Dornier Bombers
RAF in Germany

Vintage Aircraft
German Naval Air Service
Sopwith Camel
Fleet Air Arm, 1920–1939
German Bombers of WWI

Soldiers
World War One: 1914
World War One: 1915
World War One: 1916
Union Forces of the American
 Civil War
Confederate Forces of the
 American Civil War
Luftwaffe Uniforms
British Battledress 1945–1967
 (2 vols)

Warships
Japanese Battleships, 1897–
 1945
Escort Carriers of World War
 Two
German Battleships, 1897–
 1945
Soviet Navy at War, 1941–1945
US Navy in World War Two,
 1943–1944
US Navy, 1946–1980 (2 vols)
British Submarines of World
 War One

Military Vehicles
The Chieftain Tank
Soviet Mechanized Firepower
 Today
British Armoured Cars since
 1945
NATO Armoured Fighting
 Vehicles
The Road to Berlin
NATO Support Vehicles

The *Illustrated* series

The internationally successful range of photo albums devoted to current, recent and historic topics, compiled by leading authors and representing the best means of obtaining your own photo archive.

Warbirds
US Spyplanes
USAF Today
Strategic Bombers, 1945–1985
Air War over Germany
Mirage
US Naval and Marine Aircraft
 Today
USAAF in World War Two
B-17 Flying Fortress
Tornado
Junkers Bombers of World War
 Two
Argentine Air Forces in the
 Falklands Conflict
F-4 Phantom Vol II
Army Gunships in Vietnam
Soviet Air Power Today
F-105 Thunderchief
Fifty Classic Warbirds
Canberra and B-57
German Jets of World War Two

Vintage Warbirds
The Royal Flying Corps in
 World War One
German Army Air Service in
 World War One
RAF between the Wars
The Bristol Fighter
Fokker Fighters of World War
 One
Air War over Britain, 1914–
 1918
Nieuport Aircraft of World War
 One

Tanks
Israeli Tanks and Combat
 Vehicles
Operation Barbarossa
Afrika Korps
Self-Propelled Howitzers
British Army Combat Vehicles
 1945 to the Present
The Churchill Tank
US Mechanized Firepower
 Today
Hitler's Panzers
Panzer Armee Afrika
US Marine Tanks in World War
 Two

Warships
The Royal Navy in 1980s
The US Navy Today
NATO Navies of the 1980s
British Destroyers in World
 War Two
Nuclear Powered Submarines
Soviet Navy Today
British Destroyers in World
 War One
The World's Aircraft Carriers,
 1914–1945
The Russian Convoys, 1941–
 1945
The US Navy in World War
 Two
British Submarines in World
 War Two
British Cruisers in World War
 One
U-Boats of World War Two
Malta Convoys, 1940–1943

Uniforms
US Special Forces of World
 War Two
US Special Forces 1945 to the
 Present
The British Army in Northern
 Ireland
Israeli Defence Forces, 1948 to
 the Present
British Special Forces, 1945 to
 Present
US Army Uniforms Europe,
 1944–1945
The French Foreign Legion
Modern American Soldier
Israeli Elite Units
US Airborne Forces of World
 War Two
The Boer War
The Commandos World War
 Two to the Present
Victorian Colonial Wars

A catalogue listing these series and other Arms & Armour Press titles is available on request from: Sales Department, Arms & Armour Press, Artillery House, Artillery Row, London SW1P 1RT.